# LIFE with
# MAMA ROSIE

# LIFE with
# MAMA ROSIE

*A Memoir*

Sandra L. Fluker

# LIFE WITH MAMA ROSIE
# A MEMOIR

Scripture quotations marked KJV are from the Holy Bible, King James Version
(Authorized Version). First published in 1611. Quoted from the KJV Classic
Reference Bible, Copyright © 1983 by The Zondervan Corporation.

iUniverse books may be ordered through booksellers or by contacting:

iUniverse
1663 Liberty Drive
Bloomington, IN 47403
www.iuniverse.com
1-800-Authors (1-800-288-4677)

ISBN: 978-1-5320-2177-0 (sc)
ISBN: 978-1-5320-2178-7 (e)

Library of Congress Control Number: 2017905869

Print information available on the last page.

iUniverse rev. date:    08/12/2017

# Dedications

I would like to dedicate this book
to my beloved children:
Timothy, Selena, Melonie, and Myra—
For their unconditional love
and support all your lives
-for my beloved husband Clarence,
now resting with the Lord, who
also loved me unconditionally
To my dear friend in the Colony, Freddie Lee
Porter who has always been there for me
To Grandmothers everywhere
Who have loved and provided for their
children and their children's children
To my beloved sister Loisetta Hodge who
has raised her grandchildren from birth in
the fear and admonition of the Lord.
To my granddaughter Bria who was born
on my birthday. And my baby sister Angel
who has gone to be with the Lord

# *Preface*

My name is Sandra Laverne and my mother intended for my nickname to be Vonnie for Laverne. But everyone would call me Bonnie instead; so that is how I got the nickname, Bonnie. I have wanted to write this book about my grandmother for a long time. I want to introduce her to the world, for one of such notable character and her many attributes should be known. Mama Rosie was the center of everything that was good. Her life was a life of service. She was a provider for all of her children and grandchildren. She never complained as the grandchildren kept coming. She just rolled up her sleeves and took care of all of us. She was indeed the epitome of the virtuous woman in the book of Proverbs; kind, caring, full of love for God and man. She was a source of wisdom and security. She was the first to teach me about Jesus and His great love.

All my life I have tried to emulate every aspect of her character.

*Her children arise up, and call her blessed*
*Her husband also*
*Many daughters have done virtuously,*
*But thou excels them all*

# *Life with Mama Rosie*

Some of the happiest years of my life, as a child were spent with my grandmother, Rosie Staton, who we affectionately called Mama Rosie. She lived in a small country town called "The Colony." I often wondered what my life would have been like if I hadn't spent the most important years of a child's life with her, those formative years. I used to wonder also, how my mother could leave her five month old baby with in laws she had just met. As I got older I realized it must have been divine providence for her to make that choice because life with my young parents later was quite a contrast to the life I had experience with my grandmother. My grandmother gave me the foundation that I needed to succeed in every area of my life and my life with her truly defined me. Someone once said that a grandmother-grandchild relationship is simple: Grandmas are short on criticism and long on love. That couldn't be more of the truth in describing my grandmother. In addition to raising me from five months to the age of about four years old, my younger brothers came down to stay with her also during the summer months. Several times we all stayed for the school year. Visiting our grandmother was the highlight of our lives and I will always love the Colony.

The Colony is located about 50 miles north of Birmingham, AL and was actually part of another small town called Hanceville Arkadelphia. Both were products of Cullman County, Alabama. This area in Alabama was founded in about 1871 and has a very rich history. It was inhabited for many years by various cultures of indigenous people. The historic Cherokee and Choctaw lived here at the time of the European Encounter. It's interesting to note that the Cherokee, who remained in the county after the Indian Removal in the 1830's have worked at reviving their culture in the last 30 years.

It is believed that Colony, Alabama, was originally settled after the Civil War during Reconstruction and following the emancipation or the freedom of slaves. The people that came to live in the area had probably been freed slaves from the old settlement of Baltimore, AL. It is Cullman County's only African American community and in the early days, it was considered a safe haven for African American slaves in the Deep South. Major Reid, a former slave, was one of the first people to settle in Colony. He received his land as compensation for unknown services. His brother, Enoch Montgomery, also a former slave, received his land by filing a claim in Huntsville, AL. Reid died in 1893 and Montgomery died in 1894. The brothers are buried in the Pleasant Grove United Methodist Church cemetery in Colony. This is the only cemetery in Colony and Mama Rosie and many other relatives are buried there today right behind the church.

# Who Was Mama Rosie

My grandmother was a most unusual person. She was noble and so virtuous. She was the epitome of the Proverbs Woman in the book of Proverbs 31 in the King James version of the Bible:

*Who can find a virtuous woman?*
*For her price is far above rubies*
*She seeketh wool, and flax, and*
*worketh willingly with her hands.*
*She is like the merchants' ships; she*
*bringeth her food from afar.*
*She riseth also while it is yet night,*
*and giveth meat to her household.*
*She girdeth her loins with strength,*
*and strengtheneth her arms.*
*She perceiveth that her merchandise is*
*good; her candle goeth not out by night*
*She layth her hands to the spindle,*
*and her hands hold the distaff.*

*She stretcheth out her hand to the poor; yea,*
*she reacheth forth her hands to the needy.*
*She is not afraid of the snow for her household;*
*for all her house hold are clothed with*
*Scarlet.*
*She maketh herself coverings of tapestry;*
*her clothing is silk and purple.*
*Strength and honour are her clothing;*
*and she shall rejoice in time to come*
*She looketh well to the ways of her household,*
*and eat not the bread of idleness.*
*Her children arise up, and call her blessed;*
*her husband also, and he praise her*
*Many daughters have done virtuously,*
*but thou excellest them all*
*Favor is deceitful, and beauty is vain; but a*
*woman that feareth the Lord, she shall be praised*
*Give her of the fruit of her hands; and let*
*her own works praise her in the gates.*

There was never a more noble, gentle, and kinder soul that have walked this Earth than my grandmother. She was affectionately called, Mama Rosie by her grandchildren. She was known far and near for her serene calm spirit and words of wisdom for everyone. She seldom talked, or got angry or raised her voice, but when she did she always got results. She was a beautiful woman with Indian features; long black hair, medium build with light brown complexion, and a smile that would light up any dark room. My grandfather was equally handsome, with straight brown hair, blue eyes, medium frame, and very light complexion. In fact, he looked white. My grandmother was quite a bit younger than my grandfather when they married and moved to the Colony. They had six children, three girls and three boys. They also had a seventh child who had died as a young child. Their children were known to be extremely good looking. My aunts were beautiful, the epitome of what every little black girl at that time wanted to look like, with light complexion and long flowing hair. How I used to love to comb their hair. In my little world, long hair defined the whole person— surely you had no problems if you had hair like theirs. In addition to being so beautiful, they were equally talented. All three could sing like angels, especially the youngest daughter. When they were teenagers they traveled all over the world singing with this gospel group. They were quite famous and successful. They rubbed shoulders with many famous people back then, like, Sam Cooke, Mahalia Jackson, Lou Rawls,

The Staple Singers, and even Mary McCleod Bethune, founder of Bethune-Cookman College. The youngest daughter was also a very prolific song writer. Gosh, we were so proud of them all.

My father was the oldest, and while still in his teens, he had gone into the army. While on leave in Cleveland, OH, he met my mother, they got married, and I was born soon afterwards. I thought my father was the most handsome man alive. He took his new bride and baby to meet his family in the Colony, Alabama when I was five months old. My grandmother told me years later how she had jokingly ask my young mother if she could keep me, and to her surprise, my mother wholeheartedly consented. She said she still could hardly believe it but several days later, my parents drove off without me at five months old leaving me there with my grandparents. Well, I was pampered by everyone. My life during those early years with my grandparents, were very happy years. I was the baby in the house in every sense of the word. I can still remember some things being yet a baby, like sitting on the bedroom floor with a large jar of Vaseline hair grease rubbing it in my hair and my grandmother coming in picking me up in her arms with this big smile on her face and saying, "Lord, look at my baby." I remember also this picture of the Lord's Supper which hung over the door leading into the kitchen. I would stand for the longest just staring at that picture. Years later when I shared these memories with her, she was astonished and said I was no more than 18 months old. I stayed with them until the age of about three or four, then my parents came and took me back to Cleveland, OH.

# Life in the Colony

Colony was and still is a very small town. In fact, at the 2014 census, the population was approximately 385 and even less when I was a child. Everyone knew everyone else and their history even to this day.

It was a very small community where everyone's social structure was about the same. The small homes were scattered far apart. Most of the people who lived there were farmers. They grew their own food and a few men worked in the coal mines also, like my grandfather. My grandmother lived in a small four room house. Even though the house was small and sparsely furnished with the barest of necessities, it was booming with so much love and activity most of the time. She kept the house spotless. I mean everything had its place; in spite of the fact that there would be at times up to eleven or twelve people in the house. Anything that was taken out of place in Mama Rosie's house had to be put back in its place. She kept our little humble home immaculate. Even though it has been many years ago, I still have vivid memories of our little home. I mean every detail of where all the furniture was placed. In the living room was the little black pot-bellied wood burning stove that kept the house warm. Next to it was a double bed and on the other side of the room was the large big screen television set; a cabinet was next to it with our prize possession on top, the radio. How we love to listen to the radio. The only music we were allowed to listen to were gospel and country western music. I loved them both. I can remember listening to the lyrics of these country western songs. The lyrics in these songs would just come alive as my imagination soared placing myself dead smack in the middle of each song's adventure or situation. Most of these country western songs were about the singer's long lost loves and were so vivid and imaginative.

The gospel music was uplifting and full of life. Sometimes when Mama Rosie would go into town or visit neighbors, my uncle would change the station to the pop music and we would sing and dance to the latest tunes, careful to look out for her return. The two bedrooms were furnished with beds and several dressers and included a roll-away bed that I slept on. In Mama Rosie's room there was also a sewing machine and it had a foot peddle for stitching and the faster she would peddle it with her foot, the faster it would stitch. I can see her now sitting there sewing away. The kitchen also had a wood burning stove that she cooked on. During meal time, we would all sit at this table with long benches on both sides. There was also an old ice box in the kitchen and the ice man would come and bring this huge block of ice which went inside the top of the ice box to keep the food cold. These were the days before electricity in the nineteen fifties.

We had farm animals that we so adored. There were pigs, a cow, chickens, dogs, and several cats. Some of the happiest days of my life were those summers we spent with our grandparents. I still remember the long drives from Cleveland to the Colony. We would stop by the side of the road and eat the fried chicken and other food my mother had prepared for the trip. There were no seat belts back then and I would stand up in the back seat area and gaze out the front window as my father drove mile after mile. I remember thinking how smart my father was to know the way from Cleveland, OH to my grandmother's house in Alabama. I was too young to realize he was following road signs for directions. It seemed as if we would never get there. We would go to sleep, wake up, and go back to sleep again several times until we finally arrived. Oh, what joy it would be to see my grandmother again and all the farm animals and our old friends!

Life on the farm was simple and routine. Every morning Mama Rosie awoke early to prepare breakfast. We would awake to the smell of bacon, eggs, salmon croquettes, grits, biscuits, coffee for the adults, and milk for us children. After breakfast and chores, Mama Rosie would start her daily routine and we children were allowed to rump and play on the farm. After dinner during the summer months after sun down, we would sit out on the front porch. All the animals would have gone underneath the house, the chickens, dogs, cats, all under there together. It's amazing how well they all got along. The dogs never fought the cats and neither ever bothered the chickens. They just went about their business each and every day as animals do. Sometimes late at night my brothers and I would look down through the cracks of the floor in the house and we could see them lying underneath the house.

Sometimes they would peer back up at us. Mama Rosie would sit in the porch swing with maybe one or two other adults and we children would sit on the porch floor or steps listening to the grownups talk. They would talk usually about the latest news circulating around the Colony. Every now or then a passer- by would stop and chat a while.

Sometimes they would talk about ghost stories. How we love to hear them talk about ghost stories. Mama Rosie was the ultimate story teller especially when she would tell of her many encounters with ghosts. Her voice would rise and lower as she went from one monotone to another describing those ghostly encounters. We kids would sit paralyzed with fear as she shared one tale after another. Occasionally a neighbor would also share a ghost story and we would be equally frightened. It would be black dark outside with just the kerosene lamp in the window and sometimes only the moon for light. Heaven help us if we had to use the restroom. We would shake with fear all the way there and back. This was the nineteen fifties and we didn't have inside restrooms. We were in the south and had to go outside to the outhouse to use the restroom. Mama Rosie kept an old jug in the back room for us children to use at night. We would always accompany each other, never alone and still we would be afraid. When it was time for us to go to bed, we had to wash our feet in this small white basin and brush our teeth. After prayer, we would crawl into bed. We would lie there in bed recounting each and every detail of each horrid ghost story and if we heard any unfamiliar sounds such as cracks in the floors or unusual noises from the outside, under the covers my brothers and I went. We were so afraid that we didn't mind the intense heat and somehow we'd fall asleep. Sometimes those ghost tales would become part of my dreams. It's amazing that even though these stories frightened us beyond measure, listening to these stories still fascinated us.

After dinner during the winter months, we would sit around the little wood burning, pot-bellied stove and just talk, usually about the events of the day. Often times she would turn on the radio and we would listen to gospel music. I still remember the gospel greats of that time, like The Five Blind Boys, Mahalia Jackson, Sam Cooke, the Soul Stirrers, and The Clara Ward Singers, just to name a few. I could see even as a small child how this music really affected

Mama Rosie. She would clap her hands, throw her head back, and sing to her heart's content. Other times she would become very emotional and close her eyes, and just sway back and forth to the music. Her actions dictated all of our actions. We just flowed with her moods. The little pot-bellied stove would warm the whole house, and early winter mornings, she would arise very early and start the fire in that old wood burning stove. By the time we were up and about, the house would be so warm. The smell of bacon, eggs, coffee, and other goodies coming from the kitchen, made getting out of the nice warm bed a treat. When my brothers and I were older we had a television and we would watch TV in the evenings. Mama Rosie would bring out roasted peanuts or some other snack and we'd watch such favorites as The Lone Ranger, Roy Rogers, I Love Lucy, Ed Sullivan, and my favorite, Father Knows Best. When my brothers and I stayed the school year, we'd come home after school and watch the Mickey Mouse Club. We sure did love the Musketeers. My brothers and uncle loved Annette Funicellow -- my idol was handsome Bobby. We could name all the Musketeers too.

My grandmother love to plant flowers and our front yard was always beautifully kept. I mean picturesque perfect. I can still vision the front yard with the beautiful green grass and flower beds lined on both sides of the yard. Some of the flowers were planted in old tires painted white with zig zag designs cut around the edges. At the front of the yard were green hedges on both sides of the walk-way separating the yard from the dusty road. She would take tree branches and tie them together to make a broom to sweep the yard. The yard was just lovely. All along the sides of the house were apple and peach trees. There were also persimmon trees. How we love persimmons. The only thing about this fruit was, if you bit into one that was not quite ripe, it felt like your mouth was being drawn up, and it took a while for your mouth to feel normal again, but when they were good and ripe, oh my, were they good! They were so sweet and tasty, similar to ripe delicious peaches.

My grandparents would farm an array of vegetables and fruits out in the fields, such as okra, potatoes, corn, beans, tomatoes, and when I was very young, they even planted cotton. The most interesting plant of all was the peanut plant. These plants were planted in rows and they looked simply like green weeds growing, but when you pulled the plants out of the ground, there were all these peanuts at the end of the plants. I learned later that the peanuts were actually the roots of the plant. They were so amazing. She would roast the peanuts in the oven and we would sit around in the back yard eating roasted peanuts and chatting about whatever was going on in the Colony. Sometimes she would roast corn on the cob or sweet potatoes.

Another interesting plant was the cotton plant. I would watch my grandparents, aunts, and uncles head for the fields early in the morning to pick cotton with their cotton sacks over their necks. I never will forget when my grandmother finally allowed me to go and pick cotton. She took an old empty flour bag and made me a little cotton sack and put it around my neck and off I went. Well, I remember picking cotton wasn't as exciting as I thought; the bulbs would stick your hands as you pulled the cotton out, and the early morning dew on the ground was wet, and the bugs sure would bite. I hated it. I never ask her again.

Years later when I was older, my brothers and I had to pick cotton but we got paid for it. Picking cotton was hard work. You had to bend over to the height of the cotton plant, pick the cotton and put it in your cotton sack, then drag the sack down these long rows. It was tedious work and I truly hated it. Little girls didn't wear pants back then; we had to wear dresses or skirts with bobby socks and in the early morning the ground would be wet from the dew and the wet cotton plants would rub against our legs as we pick the cotton and the bugs would surely bite without reservation--these were the days before insect spray. By the late nineteen fifties, my grandparents had stopped planting cotton and we picked cotton for a man named Mr. Johnny Johnson. He would come and pick us up before dawn in his old red pick-up truck. We'd all hop on the back of his truck with our sacks. We'd pick cotton all day until the late afternoon. The pay back then was two dollars per hundred pounds of cotton picked. That was quite a lot of money back then. I could never pick no more than sixty to seventy pounds all day and sometimes I'd make a whooping dollar fifty. That was almost six dollars a week if I worked every week day. Even though the sack was uncomfortable around my neck, the bulbs from the cotton plant would stick my hands, and the bugs would bite, the thought of getting paid motivated me to keep picking. We'd start out even—I could only handle one row at a time, everyone else would pick from two rows, first one side then the other. I was always the last one to finish even though I only picked from one row. I was no cotton picker. At the end of the day we would get our cotton sacks weighed on this large scale attached to his truck and Mr. Johnson would pay us cash money for our labor. Back then, money was quite scarce, especially for us kids; maybe we would get a nickel or if we were lucky, a dime every now and then from someone, but to have five or six dollars at one time! WOW!!!

## The Peddler Man

"Here comes the Peddler Man," my uncle or I would yell. Every weekday around noon, this huge truck would come through the Colony-it was a store on wheels driven by this middle age very kind white man. His coming was the highlight of our day. He sold everything from household goods, farm and garden tools, and groceries. The Colony only had two small stores that sold only a minimum of goods, so the Peddler Man was a welcome sight. He even sold personal and medical supplies. We loved the Peddler Man. To us youngsters he was simply "The Cracker Jack Man." A box of cracker jacks was only ten cents and oh how we loved this treat! There were no other treat like it and it was like getting three treats in one. In addition to getting this crispy caramel popcorn and peanuts, there was always a toy in the bottom of the box! Even the box didn't go to waste when it was empty. We would cover the opening with our mouths and blow as hard as we could, and wella, we had a horn! We never knew when Mama Rosie was going to buy us a box of cracker jacks or some other treat. We would stand there with much expectation. If she didn't buy us treats, we did not lose faith because there was always tomorrow and the prospect of getting these treats really motivated us to complete our chores. Another favorite was the Babe Ruth candy bars. They too were ten cents and twice as large as they are now. The promise of these treats would motivate us to do any task and do it well.

I have such fond memories of the Peddler Man. When I returned to the Colony at age twelve, the first thing I wanted to know was if he still came, and to my delight, he did. We would save our money from picking cotton for the Peddler Man when we got older. I will never forget his kind smile, generosity, and hearty laugh and he and Mama Rosie would talk for the longest time. Sometimes he would give us these red and white pepper mint candy sticks for free. He was such an awesome part of our lives. My grandmother later told me he stopped coming around the mid- sixties. By then, almost everyone had automobiles and electricity. It was good-by also to the ice man who brought huge blocks of ice to put inside the top of our ice box to keep the food from spoiling, because by then we had an electric refrigerator and television.

# The Faithful Well

"Mama Rosie, what would happen if I let the bucket down in the well and there would be no water?" I remember asking her once, "Well," she replied, "It has never ran dry before, there has always been water in our well, the Lord makes sure of that," she'd say. We had heard of other people's wells going dry, but ours never did. The water from the well was always so good and so cold, no matter how hot the weather was. It was my brothers and my job to draw water from the well when needed. Drawing water was a challenging job. There was this long chain with a bucket at the end of it. You had to slowly lower the bucket down into the well by the chain. When the bucket would fill full of water, you had to pull it back up by the chain. You had to pull the bucket up slowly and carefully. If not, the chain could get off track and you would have to let the bucket drop back down into the well, re-adjust the chain back on the track and pull the bucket of water back up and empty it into the drinking bucket. There were always two drinking buckets to fill and when you could carry both buckets, one in each hand back to the house, that was quite an accomplishment. I was about eight years old when I finally could master that feat. I felt such a sense of pride, why that was one less thing my brothers had on me. Why, I could already out run them both and beat them at wrestling. In addition for drinking, the well water was used for everything, cooking, bathing, watering the plants, everything. It was indeed one of our main life sources and there was always water in our well. Now, of-course she would use large containers to collect water when it rained but when it didn't, we could always depend on our faithful well. It still sits there today but not in use, having been replaced by "running water from the faucet."

# *Our Animals*

We had different animals at various times on the farm. Sometimes we had hogs, even a cow and a horse. We always had dogs and cats, and chickens. I still remember our dogs. There were Bullet, Shadow, and Spotty. The dogs were amazing and had their own distinct personalities. Shadow was the best looking; he was all white with a few brown spots here and there. He was rather insidious and aggressive. He didn't like to be cuddled and petted and he stayed his distance, very aloof. He seldom mingled with the other two. When Bullet and Spotty would play together in the yard, Shadow, most times, would be off to himself. Bullet was all black. He was an older dog. He was so sweet but very territorial and protective of the family. Once when my brother and I were play wrestling in the back yard, Bullet lit into my brother trying to protect me. Little

Spotty was the baby of the three. He was so passive and vulnerable and loved to be cuddled. We had to really watch out for Spotty, especially during feeding time because Shadow was forever attacking him and trying to take his food. Bullet, however, would fight. In spite of the fact that Bullet was older and a little slower, he still held his own. Shadow never bothered him.

My brothers and I stayed the school year a couple of times in the Colony. Across the road from our house was a half mile of flat land and then there were the forest on both sides of the road. Those dogs would follow us each morning on our way to school until we got to the forest and for some reason, they would stop and go no farther. They would simply stand there wagging their tales until we got out of site. Every day, after school on our way home, there they would be, right in the same place waiting for us. It was so amazing that they knew what time we came home each day. "When I see them take off down the road every evening, I know you children are coming," said Mama Rosie often. I can still see them now, jumping up and down barking their heads off as we came down the road. Those days were such happy memories and how we loved those dogs.

We always had chickens too. Once we even had a couple of turkeys. It was my brothers and my job to feed the chickens and the other animals. My grandmother kept a slop pail in the back yard on the side of one of the steps and all the left over food no matter how old and stale went into that slop pale for the hogs. The smell would be horrific at times. My brothers or uncle had to carry it to the hog pen for the hogs and those hogs would go at that slop like it was steak and gravy. They were our only animals that I did not like; they were ugly and so dirty and smelly. That is about all I remember about those hogs.

One thing I'll never forget as long as I live was when I saw my uncle wring a chicken's neck for us to eat at dinner time. He would catch this poor chicken by the neck and wring it around and around until its head came off. The other chickens would flee underneath the house. The headless body of this poor creature would take off running across the yard and the head, detached from the body, would be jumping up and down on the ground by itself. It was some gruesome site. I was only about seven years old the first and only time I saw this and I remember running and screaming across the road almost in utter shock. My uncle came running after me calling my name. I heard him calling me but I couldn't stop running and screaming. He finally caught up with me and brought me back to the house in total hysteria. My beloved grandmother embraced me and held me on her lap rocking me back and forwards with soothing words. Mama Rosie seldom passed up an opportunity to use certain incidents as teachable moments and this one horrific incident was no exception. I remember her telling me the story from the Bible about the Children of Israel; when they were in the wilderness and wanted meat to eat instead of the manna God had provided. God sent birds called quale from heaven that flew straight into their hands for them to eat. The birds gave them strength and energy for their journey. She explained that all their lives we had fed and protected them and she believed that just maybe the chickens knew that one day they would have to provide themselves as food for us and perhaps that is why they never ran away even though they saw one of their own die. It was indeed a teachable moment and I never forgot her telling me this, it helped some but not a lot. I mean for days I visualized that headless animal running across the yard and saw its head, detached from the body, jumping up and down. It really left a lasting impact on me for years. I still cringe even now thinking about that day. But, during dinner when she put that plate of crispy fried chicken on the dinner table, it just did not relate or connect to that headless creature running across the yard!

# *Laundry Day*

Mama Rosie was very organized and had a routine for most of her chores. Laundry day was no exception. When I was very young we would go down to the spring to wash our clothes. She would load several bundles of dirty clothes in sacks and with our round tin tub and scrub board and of course detergent, off to the spring we would go on foot. We had so much fun walking along the dusty road singing, playing tag, or just talking. When we got there we would fill the tin tub full of spring water and detergent and using the scrub board, they would take turns scrubbing the clothes. The clothes were rinsed with water from the spring, loaded up, taken back home, and hung on the lines. Mama Rosie would boil the sheets and other white clothes in this large black pot on the side of the house until they were white as snow. She would put coal and wood underneath the pot to keep it boiling. She'd rinse the sheets in the large tin tub filled with well water and hang them on the lines. Gosh, those clothes would smell so good coming off those lines when they were dry. Years later, we got a wringer type washing machine and did that make laundry day so much easier. "Be careful baby don't get your hands caught in the wringer," she would say. How I loved sending the clothes through the wringer. I felt so grown up. The large tin tub full of well water would catch the clothes, rinse them, and we would send them back through the wringer and hang them up on lines. She still used the large black pot to boil her white sheets, however. Sometimes when the clothes lines got old, she would give them to us and we would use them to play jump rope.

# Canning Day

As I stated earlier, we farmed many fruits and vegetables during the summer. To have an ample supply of food for the winter, my grandmother would can much of our food during harvest. There would be peaches, pears, apples, jellies, corn, tomatoes, squash, pickles, beans, okra, and peas for canning. This was usually an all day job. It involved, placing foods in mason jars and heating them to destroy the germs that cause food to spoil. During the heating process air is driven out of the jars as they would cool and a vacuum seal is formed which prevents air from getting back into the jars and germs which could contaminate the food. It had to be done correctly to prevent food poisoning. My brothers and I had to draw bucket after bucket of water to have enough water. I can still remember the myriad of canned jars of fruits and vegetables lined on the kitchen pantry shelves and some were even on the bedroom floor next to the kitchen.

Sometimes during harvest when there were an abundance of fruit and vegetables, my grandparents would sell the produce at the market in Birmingham. We would load all the food in boxes and off we would go to the market. By then we had an old truck and my brothers and I would jump on the back and my uncle would do the driving. Mama Rosie would sit up front with my uncle. We could hear her from time to time cautioning him to slow down; he had just recently learned to drive and he just loved it. Those trips to the market were so much fun. "Don't you kids eat all that fruit out those boxes," she would yell! She really didn't mind us eating the fruit because there was so much of it. It usually didn't take long to sell the produce, but we had so much that we would be there sometimes until dark. One incident I will never forget at the market. This was the nineteen fifties and when we had to use the rest room, we had to go all the way around the back of the building. There were signs directing colored people where to go to use the restrooms. There were three restrooms, one for white females, another for white males, and only one restroom for both colored men and women way around the back. I'll never forget those signs. The smell was horrible and there were no lights in the colored restroom so we had to feel our way around to find the commode when it was dark outside. There was no door for privacy so we each had to take turns standing in the doorway while the other used the restroom for privacy. That night as I lay in bed I couldn't help but cry as I visualized my beloved Mama Rosie feeling her way around in that tiny little smelly restroom for the commode. It was heart-breaking. I couldn't fathom anyone thinking she was not good enough to use their restroom.

I can remember seeing those same signs when we would go into town to Cullman or Birmingham to shop. They were in front of the restaurants, water fountains, and some other businesses. The races were definitely segregated back then, but we were much too young to understand the significance of all its implications and my grandparents never really talked about it when we were children. It was seemingly the accepted way of life. I'll never forget the time we were shopping in this clothing store in Cullman. There was this little white girl who kept staring at me. Everywhere I went in that store, her eyes would follow me. She made me feel very uncomfortable and I wondered about my appearance. Maybe it was my clothes or my short kinky hair which was quite a contrast to her long beautiful brown hair. I told my grandmother about it and she said that perhaps this child had never seen a little colored girl and not to worry about it and to stay quiet and close to her side. When we finally got in line to pay for our goods she and her mother were leaving the store and as she was going out the door, she turned, looked straight at me, and did the most unexpected thing, she smiled; the most beautiful, brightest smile ever. I was shocked. I don't remember if I smiled back; I don't think so, but I sure did feel better. Her smile was real; I could tell even then. I have never forgotten that child and her bright smile that day in Cullman, Alabama.

# Schools Days

My brothers and I were really happy to stay with Mama Rosie during the school year several times. She would pack our lunch the night before which usually consisted of a large thick piece of bologna and biscuits and sometimes a piece of cake. Sometimes we would have peanut butter and crackers. Early at dawn, we would awake to the smell of bacon, eggs, biscuits, and grits and the radio blaring with country western or gospel music. It would be fall season and sometimes the weather was quite cool. Mama Rosie or my grandfather would always arise especially early to start a fire in the old wood and coal burning stove. The house was always nice and warm by the time we got up. After breakfast off we went to school walking along that long dusty road, up and down one hill then another. The old school house was about a mile and half from our house but seemed so much longer then. The children who lived in Hanceville or along the highway would ride the school bus. How I used to want to ride on that bus, but we had to walk to school.

We were well aware of the wrath of the principal if we were late, so we never wasted time playing along the way but hurried up and got to school. In his office, there were always an ample supply of switches and a paddle which he did not hesitate to use. Back then in the fifties and sixties, teachers and principals could physically punish students and I can remember getting the switch several times. What a difference school is now days; teachers aren't even allowed to raise their voices in the classroom. School always started with prayer back then. We would stand around the little pot- bellied stove in the middle of the room in a circle and say the Lord's Prayer, then we would sing some song about Abraham Lincoln. I cannot remember the words to that song only something about him being good and brave. If it was a holiday, we would sing holiday songs. The school house was built up high and we could go underneath it and play or eat our lunch doing lunch time.

There were always animals around the school house, chickens, dogs and cats waiting to share our lunch. There were only three classrooms—one for the elementary students, one for the middle school or upper elementary, and then down the hall, a classroom for the high school students.

The classrooms were very plain and simple. We sat at long tables with benches; there were the teacher's desk and chair, the round pot- bellied stove in each classroom, and blackboard. The only book I remember reading were the Dick and Jane books. I will never forget those books or the dog in the story. His name was Spot and it puzzled me that the sound he made in the story was "bow wow, bow wow." I was in first grade and as I read, I remember thinking that dogs did not bark like that, but the sound they made was "woof woof". Years later when I became a teacher I noticed the authors of children's books now indeed have dogs in the stories making the correct barking sounds of "woof- woof." Some things you just never forget.

There was this large field in back of the school and during recess we would have to "march." We had to get in a single line just like in the army and we had to march all around that huge field. Sometimes we would march all the way back in the woods to where the Baptist church was located. We hated it. We would have rather been playing tag, hide and seek, or some other fun games. I never could understand the purpose of all that marching. Years later I ask our leader who was a high school student at the time, why did we have to do all that marching. She simply said that it was orders from the principal, who had once been in the army. The school also had a large community room where all the recreational activities, political matters, and all other meetings were held. That community room will be forever in my memory for the fun, fellowship, and food we shared during those times.

## Church Time

"Time to get up and get ready for church," was Mama Rosie's familiar call each Sunday morning. By the time we arose breakfast would be on the table and Mama Rosie up and dressed with one of her two familiar flowered white aprons on. Before long we would be off to church. We would walk that long dusty road, before we got our automobile, up one hill and down another. In the Colony, there were only two churches, the Baptist and the Methodist churches. We would take turns going to either church. I don't remember a lot about the services in either church, but I do remember liking the Baptist church more. It was lively and the preacher was more animated and there was a choir. The Methodist church was more reserved and I don't think they even had a choir and we had to walk farther to get to it. Listening to the choir sing was my favorite part of the service. The choir in the Baptist church could really sing. I mean before long the whole church would be up out of their seats, clapping their hands, and praising the Lord, even us children.

The grave-yard was in back of the Methodist church and that always gave me an eerie feeling. Sometimes during service I'd look out the window at all those graves. The only time I dared to go near it was when I had to go to a funeral. Another reason I liked the Baptist church better was because in the summer, we would have church picnics on the very grounds we had to march on during recess time in school. It was located about a quarter of a mile from the school house. In the winter we would go over to the school house community room for dinner and plays and other activities. After service, we would take that long walk back home. Sometimes, but not often, we would get a ride home.

Mama Rosie always prepared Sunday dinner on Saturday evenings. We would change our clothes and off we went to play while she prepared dinner. Sometimes we would have guest over for dinner after service. We younger folks didn't like that because we had to wait until the grown-ups ate before we could eat, especially when the preacher and his wife came for dinner. In addition to them getting the best pieces of chicken they'd sit and talk for the longest time. We children would sit on the porch pouting and angry waiting for them to leave and when they would finally leave, we could eat. It was the custom during those days for children to eat after the grownups when the preacher came for dinner. Mama Rosie always saved the dessert for us. In the summer many times it would be home-made ice cream and apple pie and sometimes we would have rice pudding and cake.

## *Christmas Time*

Christmas was so special at Mama Rosie's house. My uncle and grandfather would go out in the woods and cut down a pine tree. We would decorate the tree mostly with home-made decorations. My grandmother would always add her own decorations she had from years past with lights and other beautiful decorations. My aunts and I would make some of the decorations from whatever supplies we could find. We had a lovely tree and there were gifts underneath the tree for everyone. All around the Colony the atmosphere was so alive with the Christmas Spirit even though there was no snow. Everyone seemingly was just so happy and joyful during this time of year. On Christmas day, we would awake to the smell of turkey and dressing, and all the other holiday trimmings. My aunts made most of the desserts. They made apple and cherry pies, and several kinds of cakes and cookies. There were always plenty of nuts, candy, and fruit. Mama Rosie made sure there were gifts for everyone under the tree and the gift I received that year I'll never forget was a toy xylophone with a little stick to play it with.

On Christmas day before dinner, we'd all sit around the warm pot-bellied stove singing carols and talking about whatever. Then, we would have dinner. I can still see us all sitting on those long benches on both sides of the kitchen table. I can see the large turkey stuffed with home-made dressing, and all the other holiday dainties. There were potatoe salad, yams, green beans and other holiday goodies. What a feast and gosh, what happy times those were! We would laugh and talk until the wee hours of the night. We love listening to my aunts share their many adventures on the road singing. We sat mesmerized as they shared stories of meeting many famous people at that time and the many adventures they had on the road. They had even met Mary McCleod Bethune. She was founder of the Bethune-Cookman College in Daytona Beach, Florida and they even have a picture with her. During my college years I read everything about her that I could find. I was truly enthralled by her many accomplishments as an educator. She was one of my heroes and if I even thought about giving up school, the thought of Dr. Bethune and my beloved grandmother kept me going.

Of all the gifts I have ever received at Christmas over the years, I don't think I loved any as much as I loved that little toy xylophone. I would sit and play on it for hours. It was the first musical instrument I had ever seen other than the piano at church. I remember the very first song I learn to play on it was, "The Halls of Montezuma." That was the first of many songs I learn to play on that little toy. Singing and playing on it I believe, was what initiated my love for music; a love I instilled in my children and grandchildren. Yes, Christmas during those days were indeed special. No one in the Colony had very much materialistically, but oh, the love, peace, and security of those days. I can remember almost every detail of that Christmas day when my most beloved Mama Rosie bought me that xylophone.

# Mama Rosie

Never have a more virtuous soul graced this earth than my grandmother. I heard someone say once that there have been many more unsung heroes that have lived than heroes; that is, this world's definition of heroes. She was and is my hero. Her views on almost every facet of life were way ahead of her time and Bible oriented. She lived by the principles and teachings of Jesus Christ. I have never heard her swear or talk about anybody in a negative way. She loved the Lord and her family. I envision her now on her knees during evening prayer. Her prayers were passionate and so sincere and emotional, calling her family's names one by one and many others' names in prayer. She always took her time and prayed and her expressions were at times tearful and quiet and other times joyful and loud as she prayed from her soul. She truly instilled in us children a deep respect for God at a very early age. He had to be quite special for our grandmother to kneel down and pray to Him and talk about him so often. Whether it was cutting up a chicken or scrubbing the floors, the accolades of Jesus Christ were never far from her mouth.

Mama Rosie was the epitome of love and kindness to everyone. Even when she disciplined us, she did so with firmness and much love. Sometimes she would get the switch, but all of our infractions were used as an opportunity for a teachable moment. She taught us about heaven and hell and she never would bite her tongue as she told us the perils of hell. I remember one story she used to tell us about this little boy who was so disobedient. One day he was outside playing and his mother started calling him. He, as usual, ignored her and kept on playing. Well, suddenly the ground around him started getting red and shaking and up came this horrible looking man from out of the ground. He was red as fire and had pointed ears and horns coming out of his head and a long chain around his neck. The frightened child started running to his house. He ran and burst opened the front door to his mother screaming and yelling and pointing to the door. She couldn't understand a word he was saying. Then they heard the chains dragging the ground as the demon got closer and closer to the house. He came up the porch steps and opened the door dragging the long red chain with him as he came into the house. He stood there for a moment staring at the child and his mother. He told the child's mother that the child belonged to him and he had come to get him. He was a horror to look at with blood red eyes and long pointed fingers. He started coming towards them with his hands reaching for the child. The mother started begging for him to give her child another chance. Well, after much crying and pleading from both of them, the demon looked down at the child and said in a most fearful voice, "I'll be watching you," as he turned around and walked towards the door and left dragging that horrible red chain with him. "Well, needless to say, that mother had no more trouble out that child," my grandmother would say with that gleeful look in her eyes. Now, we were very young when she told us this story and I don't know if it was even an appropriate story to tell us children, but it sure was effective and left an indelible impression on all of us. We never forgot that story and my brothers and I love to joke about it even now. Mama Rosie would tell us about hell but never without softening the atmosphere with that wonderful story of the place called heaven. She would then proceed to talk about the story of her dear friend Job from the Bible and his notorious patience. We were introduced to him at a very young age and often.

We were always allowed to keep the money we made from picking cotton or elsewhere. She taught us the importance of spending wisely, "never waste your money, always help others, and give some to the church for the work of the Lord and you will always be blessed, and remember, God blesses them who blesses Him and His people," she admonished. Her teachable moment for that was the story of Prodigal Son, also from the Bible. This son in the story, took all his money from his inheritance and left home and spent it all on foolishness, then, he had to return home poor and hungry. Those old Bible stories left a lasting impression on us all our lives.

Back then, children were supposed to be seen and not heard, but our grandmother would always allow us to speak our thoughts and opinions and our side of every story. Even if a note was sent home by a teacher or even the principal for misbehaving in school, she would always want to hear our side of the story. "OK Bonnie," she would say to me, looking me sternly in the eyes, "let me hear your side of it." It didn't matter who the accusation were from adults or children, she always wanted to hear our side of the story. She would stare us straight in the eyes and could always tell if we were lying. Lying was our greatest offense and if we were lying, the punishment was always physical and that meant we got the switch and quite intensely. After the whipping, she would rub liniment on our little whelps and we would prepare for another teachable moment, which always came next. "Always, always, always, tell the truth and never be afraid to stand up for what is right," she would say with that very stern look on her face. "Remember, the Bible says that if you spare the rod you will spoil the child," she ended her speech warningly. We knew she meant business!

Mama Rosie taught us to pray about everything. There was a tornado once and she knew it was coming and she hurriedly made us all go into the bedroom, lie down, and pray. Tornados are terribly fearful and can do so much damage. It's amazing how the animals knew too because before the storm even came they were all under the house nice and snug. She came and knelt down beside us and all of us prayed as the storm passed through. I'll never forget the loud roaring and how the little house shook as it passed through. To say we were afraid would be an understatement. We gathered close to our grandmother and did we pray! When it was over we went outside and the only damage that was done from the tornado was an old icebox that was on the porch was thrown all the way across the field. Everything else was in place. We learned later that several of our neighbors had endured severe damages to their properties; like roofs blown off barns and some houses damaged; no one had gotten hurt however. We children saw the results of prayer at an early age and that was the only tornado I had ever witnessed.

One of my classmates used to come to school with whelps all over her body including her face. We all knew that the beatings came from her aunt she lived with. I felt so sorry for her.

She stayed to herself most of the time and always had the saddest look on her face. Her mother stayed in Birmingham and I think her father had died. When I would tell Mama Rosie about her, she simply told me to try to be very kind to her and pray for her, and that was all we could do.

I really did pray for her and eventually, her mother came and got her. I never knew what happened to her after that and I never forgot her.

Thinking about her through the years have prompt me to support several organizations for abused and neglected children also the World Vision and Smile of a Child Organizations. Another thing I remember praying fervently about when I was a child, was wetting the bed. I remember how I felt when I would wake up and the bed would be wet. I felt so badly and so ashamed. I would wake up cold and so disappointed. I mean it was something I prayed about every night. I didn't wet every night and Mama Rosie understood how I felt. She would quietly tell me to change my bed clothes and she quickly changed the bed. She didn't want the others to know because she knew how they would tease me about it. After all, I was older than my brothers. Well, I finally did stop wetting the bed after much prayer from her and me.

Mama Rosie would use such discretion and kindness, even when she disapproved of certain actions from family members. I believed I was about seven years old when this incident happened. My grandfather worked at the coal mines and he would sometimes bring his white friends over our house after work or some weekends. Now, my grandfather looked just like a white person so I assumed they just considered him one of their own—he was also very kind and friendly. Mama Rosie would fix them something to eat and they afterwards, would just sit around talking and drinking home brew. Now, I knew my grandmother absolutely did not approve of this, but she was so hospitable and kind to these people, even though I could see the disdain on her face from time to time.

One particular evening, it had gotten dark and they were still in the living room laughing and talking. This one man came over to where I was sitting and picked me up and sat me on his lap. Now, I was very uncomfortable and even frightened as he was squeezing me tightly and touching me in such an inappropriate way. I tried and tried to push his arm from around my waist and get down, but he held me tighter. I saw the look on my grandmother's face as she mouthed the words, "get down." Finally, this white man let me down and I ran into the back bedroom where my uncle and brothers were. I wanted to run back in there where my grandmother was, but he was in there. As I stood there at the end of one of the beds, feeling very confused, the man suddenly appeared in the doorway. He stared down at me for several seconds then he reached inside his pocket and brought out two dimes; I'll never forget this. He then leaned over me and offered me the money and asked me to go outside with him. My uncle jumped up, saw the money in his hand and said, "Bonnie, think what you can buy with two dimes, cracker jacks and a Babe Ruth candy bar." My young uncle had no idea what this man was up to. Thinking about what he had just done I looked at him and screamed, 'NO!" I then ran in the living room to Mama Rosie.

I truly cannot remember what happened after that but I never ever forgot that incident. All I had to do was take those two dimes, he turn that wooden latch on that side door to unlock it, and go out that door with this white man. This incident has revisited me quite often through the years especially when I heard about a child being raped or molested or even murdered, the memory of it would resurface. It has caused me much anxiety over the years. I wondered many times want would have happened to me had I gone out that door. Mama Rosie told me to pray every time I thought about it which I did and have done. I have thanked God so many times for being brave enough to say no to that man. I mean this was a white man and this happened in the fifties. This incident has given me much insight on the relationship of whites and blacks. This evil man had some nerve to ask that of me, being but a child of only about seven or eight years old and with both grandparents right there in the living room. He never would have done such a thing if we were white. A therapist told me years later how exceptionally brave I had to be being so young and standing up to this man. I credit my grandmother's example and her teaching me to always stand up for what is right no matter how afraid I might be.

The Colony was such a peaceful little community when I was a child. Everyone knew everyone else and all there was to know about each other. The only violent occurrences that I can remember back then was when several boys were coming home from the Community Center and started fighting right around the corner of the road from where we lived. Our home was located right where there was a fork in the road and one road branched off to the right down the hill and the main road continued around the bend to the left towards the mountain. We were sitting on the front porch that quite evening when we heard the young men arguing as they came down the road. There were about five or six of them and several of them went down the hill to the right and the others stayed on the main road.

We thought that was the end of it until we saw several of the boys cross the field and met back up with the others. They started fighting and all of a sudden, we saw one of them fall forward and hit the ground. He had been stabbed. Then one of the other young men came running down the road toward our house calling my uncle's name. This was the second oldest uncle who was home from the army and who had recently bought a used car. My uncle jumped in his car and ran to help. They got the wounded man to the hospital. We saw it all. That night as we lay in bed, we heard the church bells ringing and we knew this young man who had just a few hours earlier walked past our house, was dead. It was devastating for us. The only thing my young brothers and I wanted to do was stay very near my grandmother.

I still remember the strange feeling in the atmosphere. Death had come and taken away this young man's life just that quick. As I sat at his funeral, I was traumatized. I was only about 8 years old, but I still remember the pain I felt. All I could think about was just a few days ago he was walking right in front of our house with the others. He was alive. He was almost home where his mother and family members were waiting for him. He never made it. This was my first experience with the death of a person and my first funeral that I could remember. That night as I lay in bed I couldn't stop crying and thinking about the fact that he was trying to get home, he wanted to get home. Why couldn't those boys keep going down that hill? Why did the others have to cut across that field? I tried to cry silently but my grandmother heard me. "Bonnie, Bonnie, come go with me," she said ever so gently. She threw a blanket around me and we went and sat out on the front porch swing. A few seconds later, our dog Bullet came from underneath the house and sat next to us on the porch followed by my two younger brothers. None of us could sleep that night. She told us about Jesus and His crucifixion and death. How evil men had killed him and he was an innocent Man. She told me that God had brought Him back to life. "God can bring dead people back to life," I asked? "Yes He can, because, He gave us life and one day God will bring all good people who have died back to life and take them to heaven to live with Him forever," she said with that same gleeful look in her eyes and smile on her face. Boy, did I feel better and I knew it had to be true because Mama Rosie had said it. That God could indeed bring this young man back to life. We never forgot that day he died. Even now, we at times reflect on the events of that dark day. The next tragedy didn't happen in the Colony, but in Mississippi I believe, and it was the murder of a young fourteen year old black boy named Emmit Till. It still to this day also left a lasting effect on my mind. My father had bought a Jet magazine and he showed us this young man in his coffin—what they did to this child was truly inhuman. We children learned very early the dark side of mankind.

We have had several teachable moments from our beloved grandmother involving these two tragic events. We would sit around the old pot-bellied stove talking about them or out on the front porch, and I can still remember how solemn the atmosphere would become. My grandmother would always transition the conversation and console us by telling us about her favorite subject, heaven. She always left us feeling so much better and safer as she talked about that wonderful city called "New Jerusalem." The story is found in Revelation 21st chapter of the Bible. It's a literal place where there would be no more dying, crying, or even pain over there, she would say with so much joy in her eyes and that beautiful smile on her face. We would afterwards go on to bed feeling quite OK. After a while, life settled back to normal as we put these tragic events way in the back of our minds.

Shortly after that, my father came and took us back to Ohio. I was about nine at the time and I didn't return to the Colony again until I was twelve years old and the year was 1960. I rode the Greyhound bus all alone all the way down there. All I could think about on that trip was seeing my beloved Mama Rosie again. It had been almost three years since we had left the Colony. I finally arrived in Birmingham and my uncle was there to pick me up. As we neared the Colony and the old homestead, my excitement just arose. As we pulled up in the front yard, Mama Rosie came running out of the house and into her arms I went. "Why Bonnie, you are as tall as I am," she said bursting with laughter. Everything looked the same—the beautiful front yard, the flower beds, and hedges so well kept. It was such a joy to be back.

I immediately looked around for our beloved dogs. There came Bullet, walking very slow and wagging his tail; he had gotten quite a bit older and slower, but I recognized the same excitement in his eyes as he trotted over to me. I bent down and hugged him and we exchanged the same love and devotion as we had in the past. I had thought he might have forgotten me, but not my beloved Bullet. He could no longer jump up on his hind legs so he just stood there looking up at me so excitedly. "Where's Spotty and Shadow," I asked? Looking from underneath the porch was Shadow. He displayed not a sign of emotion; the same indifferent, aloof, non-chalet Shadow. I tried to coax him from underneath the porch, but he wouldn't bulge. He just laid there staring at me emptied eyed. They told me that little Spotty had just one day disappeared and he was never found. "Just like one day he appeared from nowhere, he just vanished shortly after we had left for Ohio," my uncle said. Well, anyway, it was just great being back in the Colony. My grandmother had cooked all my favorite foods. After dinner, we sat around the old stove to catch up on all the latest news.

I stayed that time for about a year. I went to school for the last time that year in the Colony. I turned 13 the following year and how excited I was at being a teenager. That morning on the way to school, I walked down the road singing, "I am a teenager now." It was some song I had made up. One of my favorite songs during those years was "Unchained Melodies." Boy, did I love that song. Sometimes I'd sing it all the way to school. For dinner that evening, Mama Rosie had baked my favorite, coconut cake and many of my favorite foods for dinner. There were candles on the cake and homemade ice cream and everyone sang happy birthday; it was so wonderful. I even received several gifts that year. I just had to save a piece of cake for Bullet and Shadow. Both of them seemed to know just what all the excitement was about as they barked and ran around the front door.

That year was 1960 and by that time the Colony had become quite modernized. Many of the residents about had automobiles, electricity, running water, and telephones. The old dusty road had been paved with black tar. No more was there dust settling for minutes after a vehicle had passed by. Mama Rosie even had an electric washing machine which made doing laundry much easier. We still had to take that long walk to school most days. We would come home from school to find her either in the kitchen cooking or sitting at the old foot peddle sewing machine, making or repairing clothes for the winter. Usually we would turn the TV on and watch the old Mickey Mouse Club until dinner was ready. As I stated, how I loved this program and I was so in love with the one named Bobby. He was one of the main Musketeers on the show. My brothers and uncle were madly in love with Annette Funicello. She was another musketeer. They sang and danced their way right into our hearts for many years. We loved all the other Musketeers and even the cartoon characters, like, Jimmie the Cricket, Pluto, and Mickey and Minnie mouse. Years later I would see Bobby dancing his heart out on the Lawrence Welk Show; still handsome as ever.

Also that year was the presidential election. The candidates were Kennedy and Nixon. As we watched the debate, Mama Rosie loved Kennedy right away. She was ecstatic when he won the presidency—we all were. He was such a good president. The Civil Rights movement was in full swing during this time and he had sent the National Guard to Birmingham to offset the rioting and protect the African Americans who were demonstrating for their basic human rights. This is just one of the many acts he performed as president. President Kennedy was concerned about and fought for the equal rights of all Americans and he didn't mind letting the world know it. He also started the Peace Corps, an organization that helped the poor all over the world. I will never forget where I was and what I was doing when he was assassinated. The year was 1963. I was in Cleveland in my high school glee club class. Someone came into class and whispered something to our teacher and he abruptly got up and left the room without saying anything. Shortly afterwards he returned and told us the president had gotten shot. Everyone gasped. I just didn't believe it and my exact words to my best friend sitting next to me were, "Awww I don't believe that----things like that don't happen these days, only in Abraham Lincoln's days." The PA system came on about that time and confirmed the news—that our beloved President Kennedy had been killed. We were totally devastated and many of the students and teachers started crying and some just stood around as if in a daze listening to their transistor radios at the news. Classes were dismissed for the next several days. I ran home and for the next four days our eyes stayed glued to the television set. Shortly after the president was killed, the man accused of killing him was shot and killed right in front of millions of people on the TV as we watched in horror. I will never forget the utter despair on Jackie Kennedy's face the first time she appeared on television following the death of her husband. In spite of it all, she displayed such dignity and bravery as she spoke. We all grieved with her. I'll never forget also the president's little son John John saluting his father as his coffin laid in state. We loved the Kennedys and always will. Our snug little world had been grossly interrupted as one catastrophic tragedy led to another. Shortly after that, our beloved Civil Rights leader Martin Luther King was assassinated and then President Kennedy's younger brother Robert Kennedy, who was running for the presidency, was killed.

There were many others like Medger Evans and Malcom X also were slain for the civil rights cause. The sixties were indeed turbulent years. There were the infamous and controversial Vietnamese War where thousands died and also the 6-Day War. But on a more positive note, the sixties brought us our very first African American mayor for a major city. The city was my hometown of Cleveland, OH and his name was Mayor Carl Stokes. He was truly an awesome mayor and we were all ecstatic with joy and so absolutely proud of him. Another noteworthy event for that era was America put its first man on the moon—the year was 1969 and I had just had my first and only son---so you can say that the sixties ended with a "bang."

One evening after my grandfather had died, Mama Rosie wanted us to go to the grave-yard to clean off his grave and plant some flowers. As I watched her on her knees planting flowers on my grandfather's grave, I became very emotional. I couldn't help but think that one day my beloved grandmother would one day be buried here also. She noticed how quiet and solemn I had become, and she momentarily stopped and looked up at me and said, "Bonnie, what's the matter? "Nothing," I replied quietly. The look in her eyes assured me that she knew what I was thinking. She stood up, smiled, and gently gave me a slight embrace and said, "Bonnie, it's going to be alright." Of course, I felt better after she said that.

I returned home that year to Cleveland at age 13 never to live in the Colony again. I had to promise her that I would "stay away from the boys" and finish high school. I remember her telling me once that because I was always so sensitive to anything that was hurt or in pain, and that I had always loved children, I would make a really good school teacher someday. I did promise her that I would be a good girl and finish high school. College was way beyond my dreams at that time and I just couldn't fathom attending it. No one had attended college in my family.

Over the years after that Mama Rosie visited Cleveland several times. The last time she visited I had gotten married and had four children of my own which included a set of twin girls. I remember taking all four of my children to see her. She was staying with my uncle who now lived in Cleveland and her second oldest son. As she looked at each one of my children so tenderly, her exact words were, "Bonnie, I never thought I'd live to see all your children." After returning home to the Colony for the last time, she became ill shortly afterwards. I went to spend some time with her and as we sat on the front porch one evening, she talked about so many things. She spoke of the Peddler Man, and how he was one of the kindest human beings she had ever known. He had shared with her that his wife had been very ill for many years and yet he would have to leave her for hours at a time to go to work driving that food truck to all the local little towns up and down one dusty road after another. "You have to do a lot of things in this old world you don't want to do to get by, putting it all in God's hands," she would say with that faraway look in her eyes.

She spoke of the young man who had gotten killed right down the road from our house. She said for years that had weighed so heavy on her heart. "If I had known that that young man was going to died like that I would have tried to stop it somehow; just didn't realize the seriousness of it all," she said with such despair and sadness in her eyes. We talked about the racial signs and the incident in the Birmingham Market when she and I had to use the separated restrooms. "It's wrong, so wrong. God never made one race of people better or superior to another. If that was so, He would not be a just and righteous God. Its man's doings and it is of the devil and one day things are going to change," she would say with that somewhat angered look on her face.

These thoughts evoked much emotion and after expressing them, she would just sit quietly and rock side to side in deep thought as she so often did in the past. I knew not to break her silence. She spoke of a time when people would have to choose which God they wanted to serve. That many would be killed if they chose Jesus Christ and Christianity. I have never forgotten these prophetic words and I have always wondered about them. This was in the seventies and I wondered if such a thing as that could happen in America where we have many freedoms, including freedom of religion.

But now as we see how this world is changing and the rise of Islam and all, could such a thing as this happen in this country as in other countries of the world where many were being killed for their religious beliefs. It was like she was prophesying indeed. She warned me never to be afraid and to stay strong and faithful in serving God. Many will not know the truth but you young people will—share what you know and remember God promises never to leave us or forsake us. Always remember also, that there are good and bad in all races of people. She reminded me of the time when we all went to pick cotton for Mr. Johnson's son and his wife. They had prepared dinner for us that evening after picking cotton all day. She had us come into their lovely home, and we sat at her dinner table and she and her young husband served us dinner. We were all somewhat shocked as they served us all this delicious food. Usually, during meal time in the cotton field, we would sit on our cotton sacks and eat the lunch we brought or bought from the Peddler. My grandmother had spoken of this couple several times during the years. It really affected her in an awesome way. "They were totally unprejudiced and had the love of Jesus in their hearts, yes, there are some mighty good God fearing people in this world," she said with that happy smile on her face. We sat there talking for seemingly hours. That was our last long talk we had together before her illness.

The next day, my aunt and I went into Cullman for lunch and shopping and afterwards we had to rush back to Mama Rosie's house because I had to finish packing. I had to catch a late evening flight back to Cleveland. As I was leaving out the door, she gave me another big embrace and said," Bonnie, I found my old hymn book and I sure was hoping we could sing some hymns before you left." I sure wanted to stay a while longer but I could not; I promised her that I would be back soon.

As my aunt and I sped along the freeway on our way to the airport, I was determined to come back that next year and spend more time with her. As the months went by, her health continued to decline. I received the phone call one day that she was in the hospital and not doing very well. I got a relative to watch my children and I left right away to be with her. When I arrived at the hospital, she was unconscious. I stayed with her day and night for the first few days. As I sat by her bedside, she was in and out of consciousness. I did for her what she had done so many times over the years for me, prayed and read the Bible. I will never forget while reading from the Bible one evening, I just happen to glance over at her and she was staring at me with a smile on her face, yes, that wonderful familiar smile. That smile that had always assured us that everything was alright and it had encouraged us so many times over the years in so many ways, and had catapulted us to keep moving forward because we had her approval. I held her hand, and kissed her on the forehead, as she drifted back into unconsciousness.

I spent the night with her and the next day, I took care of her; bathing and combing her beautiful hair just like she had done for me so many times before as a child. It was such an honor taking care of my Mama Rosie. When I got her up in a chair and was combing her hair, I couldn't help but look down at her lovely face and fought back tears as I thought about how much I loved this dear soul.

As I prepared to leave the next day, I somehow knew it would be the last time seeing her. I sure did not want to leave but I had to get back to my family. I stayed the last night there in her home and slept in her bed. By then she had a new home built and it was so lovely. The old one I had grown up in and so loved, had long since burned down. The strangest thing happened the next morning. I awoke to the sound of her voice. She was calling my name and she said, "Bonnie, look around and take whatever you want." I was the only person in the house and I recognized her voice. I knew she was in the hospital. Among her possessions I found the most wonderful book. It was a laymen's Bible commentary. It was indeed a wonderful book. I have used this book for my ministry throughout the years. It is still a valuable asset that I so cherish and I have learned so much about the Bible from reading and studying its contents. I knew my grandmother wanted me to have it. I believe with all my heart that Mama Rosie knew that one day I would be called into the ministry.

After returning home, I received the call several weeks later that she had passed away in her sleep. It was the way she had always wanted to go be with the Lord. I knew I would not go to her funeral. I was home in Cleveland with my children when she passed away. I just did not want to see my beloved Mama Rosie in a coffin. Coffins are for dead people. I knew she could never be dead. I wanted to always remember her when she was alive. I could still see her beautiful face, her hair brushed back in a bun most of the time; her smile that would light up any dark

room. I could still see her standing over that old
wood burning kitchen stove stirring food in the
pot as she prepared dinner. I could still hear her
laughter and see that far-away look in her eyes
when she was deep in thought or troubled about
something. I could still hear her praying calling
each and everyone's name and feel her warm
embrace that I was so blessed to receive from
time to time. I could hear her singing those old
gospel songs. Oh, no, my grandmother dead, no
way. She had gone to that beautiful city called
New Jerusalem that she had told us so many times
about. The city was in heaven and she was there
waiting for her children and grandchildren.

I love to reflect on her life. Never was there a
more kind, godly, virtuous and wise, person that
ever walked this earth than Rosie Staton. She
served and loved God with her whole heart. The
morals, precepts, and ways of life all were based
on biblical principles. Her righteousness reflected
in every facet of her life. I have never heard her
swear and say an unkind word about any one. Her
calm, reassuring persona would settle the most
troubled spirit. She went to church, walking the
long dusty road, read her Bible, and prayed often
and taught us the same. To see my grandmother

on her knees looking up towards heaven, praying to God like that really instilled in me a great respect and love for God throughout my life. She loved us so much. I was later told that money was seldom sent to help provide for us children from our parents, yet she provided for all of us—clothes, food, a place to stay, and never complained. One of my brothers never returned to Cleveland but spent his whole life with Mama Rosie and he is still down there living in the Colony to this day.

I remember how proud she would be over any and every one of our accomplishments—no matter how small. From teaching myself songs on my little toy xylophone, to learning to braid my own hair, to getting good grades in school, she made me feel like a queen with that big smile of pride on her face. That look of approval was such a welcome treat and really motivated us to strive to please her especially in our school work. "To become a teacher you have to make good grades," she would say. She would reward us with a Babe Ruth candy bar or box of cracker jacks from time to time for whatever we did to please her. It didn't take much at all to please her.

She was totally ecstatic when I graduated from high school, however, she couldn't make it to my graduation. I will never forget the excitement in her voice when I told her about it over the telephone. I think about how proud she would be too, to know that I did go on to college years later and became a teacher. I had had many bumps and turns in my young adult life, which included a failed marriage, but I was determined to become a teacher. I didn't start my college career until I was in my early thirties, single, with four children, and living in the projects on the west side of Cleveland. I started out at a two year community college where I graduated with an Associate of Arts Degree in Liberal Arts. It was by far the most challenging feat of my life. Remembering her encouraging words and her desire for me to become a teacher truly motivated me to make that dream a reality. It became a reality in the spring of 1991, when I graduated from Baldwin Wallace College with a Bachelor of Science Degree in Elementary Education. I later moved to Detroit and attended Wayne State University and earned my Master's Degree. Mama Rosie had passed on but somehow in my heart I knew she knew of my accomplishments and was so very proud and she was so right, teaching is my passion.

I am so thankful I was with my grandmother during my formative years when most of a child's personality has been established. Those qualities and morals she instilled in me was the guiding force throughout my life and I raised my children the same. My grandmother did not spare the rod in disciplining us and neither did I. She would be so happy to know that all my children are very successful and productive. My oldest daughter Selena, is a registered nurse, my only son Timothy is in corporate security, Melonie, the oldest twin is a Social Worker, and Myra, her twin sister is a doctor. Yes, Mama Rosie would be so happy and proud of all her children and grandchildren.

My father had passed away as a young man and it was several years before Mama Rosie passed away. Shortly after he passed, I had a dream that he came and got me in his car and took me to the old graveyard in the Colony. He took me to a grave right by the woods, not far from my grandfather's grave, and when I looked at the name on the tomb stone, it was Mama Rosie's name. When I awoke I remember feeling very sad. Well, she did pass shortly after I had that dream. I later realized I was being prepared in that dream for her demise. Years after she had passed, I went to visit my brother in the Colony, and I took a drive to the graveyard alone. I did not attend her funeral and I had no idea where her grave was located. After placing flowers on my father and grandfather's grave, I started looking for hers. I remembered in the dream that her grave was close to the wooded area and it's amazing that I found her grave, just where it was located in the dream. As I looked down at her grave, I thought about the years before as a child when she and I were just a few feet away cleaning off my grandfather's grave. I thought about the look in her eyes when she saw my sadness. She knew just what I was thinking; that one day she too would be buried right here in this very same graveyard with my grandfather.

Well, that day had come. As I looked down at her very simple grave, I didn't really feel sadness, but I felt an overwhelming thankfulness that she had been such an avid part of my life. She had passed on to me so much of her own spirit and soul. Her values of loyalty, honor, self-discipline, love, and respect for God and life and all it entailed, were all very much a part of me and still is. She had given me an impartation of all that was of her very spirit.

I truly believe Mama Rosie is going to somehow read this memoir, and when she does, I can see the smile on her face and I can hear her asking me, "Bonnie, did you do this?"